Can Science Solve?

The Mystery of the Loch Ness Monster

Holly Wallace

Heinemann Library
Des Plaines, Illinois

© 1999 Reed Educational and Professional Publishing
Published by Heinemann Library,
an imprint of Reed Educational & Professional Publishing,
1350 East Touhy Avenue, Suite 240 West
Des Plaines, IL 60018

Designed by AMR Ltd.

Cover photograph reproduced with permission of Anthony Shiels, Fortean Picture Library.

Printed in Hong Kong

03 02 01 00 99
10 9 8 7 6 5 4 3 2 1

Library of Congress Cataloging-in-Publication Data

Wallace, Holly, 1961-
    The mystery of the Loch Ness Monster / Holly Wallace.
        p. cm. – (Can science solve?)
    Includes bibliographical references (p.) and index.
    Summary: Examines the history of the Loch Ness monster story, eyewitness accounts, various efforts to discover and identify the creature, explanations for its identity, and attempts to fake its appearances.
    ISBN 1-57572-805-2 (lib. bdg.)
    1. Loch Ness monster—Juvenile literature. [1. Loch Ness monster. 2. Monsters.] I. Title. II. Series.
    QL89.2.L6W25   1999
    001.944.—dc21   98-54481
                                                                            CIP
                                                                            AC

Acknowledgments

The Publishers would like to thank the following for permission to reproduce photographs:
Express Newspapers, p.11; Fortean Picture Library, p.7; L. Coleman, p.18; R. Dahinden, p. 26; H. Gray, p.10; A. Hepburn, p. 22; I. Newby, pp. 5, 16; Project Urquhart, p. 28; A. Shiels, p. 4; D. Stacy, p.12; R. Wilson, p. 24; N. Witchell, p.15; Gamma, p. 27; Oxford Scientific Films/N. Benvie, p.13; T. Crabtree, p. 21; L. Rhodes, p.19.

Every effort has been made to contact copyright holders of any material reproduced in this book. Any omissions will be rectified in subsequent printings if notice is given to the publisher.

Some words appear in bold, **like this.** You can find out what they mean by looking in the glossary.

Contents

Unsolved Mysteries

For centuries, people have been puzzled and fascinated by mysterious places, events, and creatures. Did the lost land of Atlantis ever exist? Are UFOs tricks of the light or vehicles from outer space? Who is responsible for the mysterious crop circle patterns—clever hoaxers or alien beings? Is there really a monster living in Loch Ness? Some of these mysteries even baffle scientists. Many scientists have spent years trying to find the answers. But just how far can science go? Can it really explain the seemingly unexplainable? Are there some mysteries that science simply cannot solve? Read on, and make up your own mind.

This book tells you about the history of the Loch Ness Monster. It presents eyewitness accounts and photographic and scientific evidence. It looks at famous fakes and the different theories about whether the monster really exists. And, if it does, what type of creature it is.

This is the most famous image of the Loch Ness Monster. Is it a large, long-necked creature with a small head? This photograph was taken in 1977. It seemed to show the monster. But later, computer analysis proved it to be a fake.

What is the Loch Ness Monster?

There have been thousands of rumors and reports of mysterious monsters lurking in the world's deepest lakes. The most famous of all is the Loch Ness Monster. The word *loch* is Scottish for *lake.* Loch Ness, in the Scottish Highlands, is Britain's largest lake. It is 957 feet (290 meters) deep at its greatest depth. It is so deep that it could swallow up some of the world's tallest buildings. It is more than 300 million years old. Prehistoric rocks moved and a huge, gaping crack opened in the earth's surface. Today, monster hunters can drive around the loch on modern roads. But this was not always so. Until the 18th century, the loch was practically impossible to reach. Only remote, winding paths led there. For millions of years, a monster could have been living in the loch, hidden away.

The first modern reports of the Loch Ness Monster came in the 1930s, after a new road was built. People came carrying newly designed, easy-to-use cameras. But many of those monster photos have proven to be fakes. So, is there a monster in Loch Ness? We have thousands of eyewitness accounts of sightings. Some are more believable than others. But no traces of an actual monster have ever been found. Is there anything science can do to solve the mystery?

The murky depths of Loch Ness can now be explored by water and air. But what, if anything, does the dark water hide?

The Mystery Begins

The first accounts of the monster appeared long before roads and modern, easy-to-use cameras.

The saint and the monster

The first written report of a monster was in about A.D. 565, in the biography of the Irish saint St. Columba. It was written about a century after his death by another monk, St. Adamnan. In it he tells how one day St. Columba came to the loch to board a ferry. But the ferry was nowhere to be seen. One of Columba's followers volunteered to swim across and fetch a boat from the other side. The story says that as he dived in, a hideous monster suddenly rose to the surface and swam towards him. Everyone who saw it was "stricken with very great terror." But St. Columba saved his followers by making the sign of the cross and ordering the monster to go away. At his words, it is said, the monster turned tail and disappeared.

Searching for evidence

Most scientists are doubtful about the existence of a Loch Ness Monster. Without scientific evidence, nothing can be proved. But the nature of the loch makes finding proof extremely difficult. The first problem is its size. Loch Ness is quite big. It is the largest body of fresh water in Britain. Secondly, its water is very brown and murky. The dark water is nearly impossible to see through. Yet, people keep looking!

Water horses

Scottish folklore is full of stories of mischievous water spirits called "Kelpies." Several old books about Loch Ness tell about kelpies eating people. They are said to lurk by the lakeside. They disguise themselves as horses and wait for people to pass by. Local children were often warned not to swim in the loch for fear of the kelpies. Could the origins of the Loch Ness Monster lie with kelpies?

Kelpies were Scottish water spirits. Legend has it that they attack and eat people. The monster mystery may have sprung from folklore.

Eyewitness Accounts

Since the very first accounts, there have been 10,000 known eyewitness sightings of the monster. Although only a few have been recorded, word of mouth spread the news. The early 1930s were bumper times for sightings. The new road along the north shore of the loch made it a popular getaway sight. Here are some of the most famous sightings.

Mr. and Mrs. John Mackay

On April 14,1933, the Mackays were returning home to Drumnadrochit from a trip to Inverness. It was about three o'clock in the afternoon. A disturbance on the loch caught Mrs. Mackay's eye. She saw a large animal burst up from the water and swim to the far shore. The Mackays watched a creature with two black humps rise and fall in the water. Then it dove below the surface and disappeared. News of their sighting reached the ears of a local journalist and the Loch Ness Monster **phenomenon** was born.

Brother Richard Horan

St. Benedict's Abbey, on the shore of the loch at Fort Augustus, was home to Brother Richard Horan. On May 26, 1934, Brother Horan was working in the abbey boathouse. He heard a noise in the water. When he turned, he saw that he was being watched by a large creature with a long, graceful neck, a white stripe down its front, and a muzzle like a seal's. Other monks also reported seeing the monster.

Mr. and Mrs. George Spicer

In the summer of 1934, the Spicers were driving back to London after vacationing in Scotland. It was about four o'clock in the afternoon. About 660 feet (200 meters) ahead of them, they saw a long, dark shape stretched across the road. As they drove closer, they saw that it was a long, grey neck, followed by a grey body about five feet (1.5 meter) high. Mr. Spicer said it looked like "a huge snail with a long neck." It shot across the road with a jerky movement. Then it disappeared in a thicket of ferns. "It was horrible—an abomination," he added. After this sighting, interest in Loch Ness grew worldwide. Prizes were offered for the monster, dead or alive.

The Spicers drew a picture of the monster they had seen. It looked like no other animal.

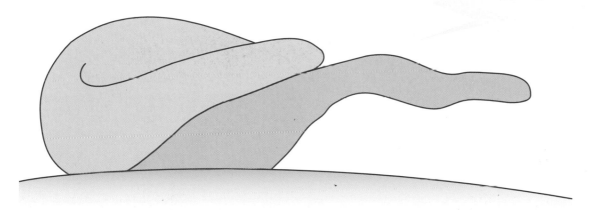

Mass Hallucinations?

Despite the number of eyewitness accounts, scientists are still suspicious. After all, they argue, people's memories often play tricks on them. Perhaps wishful thinking has a large part to play. One scientist dismissed the sightings as "a striking example of mass **hallucination**." How can all the sightings be explained?

Caught on Film

Some eyewitnesses have been able to capture the monster on film. Their photographs and home movies are greeted with great excitement. But disappointment often follows because many have turned out to be fakes.

First photograph

The first photograph of the monster, or "Nessie," was taken on November 12, 1933, by a walker, Hugh Gray. He snapped the picture as the monster rose from the water. The photo was blurry. It showed what looked like the greyish body of a large creature. The photograph was printed in two newspapers, the *Scottish Daily Record* and the *London Daily Sketch*. An expert **zoologist** from Glasgow University dismissed it. He said that it was unlike any living creature he had ever seen.

When Hugh Gray's photograph of the Loch Ness Monster was first published in 1933, it caused a huge stir. The monster quickly became known worldwide.

Three humps

Early on July 14, 1951, a local farmer, Lachlan Stuart, was milking his cows. He spotted something racing down the loch. At first, he thought it must be a speedboat. Then he noticed three large humps. He rushed inside to grab his camera. He snapped the monster from the shore.

He was only able to take one photo before his camera jammed. Many people thought that Stuart's photo was really the monster. Later, researchers concluded that it probably showed a group of rocks in shallow water near the shore.

Lachlan Stuart's photograph clearly shows three rounded shapes. Are they the humps of a huge monster? Doubters said that they were rocks.

Moving pictures

*The first movies of Nessie were taken in April 1960, by engineer Tim Dinsdale. Using a 16-mm movie camera, he took several feet of film. On film, he captured a hump swimming away from him. When played on television, the film caused a huge stir. But did it really show a monster? Six years later, the film was analyzed by British Royal Air Force Intelligence. They reported that the object was not a boat or submarine but "probably **animate**." It was also examined by computer experts at **NASA**. In addition to the main hump, they spotted two other parts that could belong to a body. Many people were convinced that this was the monster.*

It's Official!

Interest in Loch Ness continued to grow in the 1960s and 1970s. A new generation of monster seekers came on the scene. Despite the doubts of many scientists, serious expeditions were organized by universities and local biologists to search the loch for proof that the monster did or did not exist.

Since the 1930s, thousands of people have visited Loch Ness in the hope of spotting the monster. Their starting point is often the Loch Ness Visitor Center on the shore of the loch.

A full-time job

In 1969, Frank Searle of London, England, gave up his job to camp full time by Loch Ness. In 1971 his patience was rewarded. He described the monster as being "seven feet long, dark and knobby on top, smooth dirty white underneath." More sightings and a series of photographs followed. The films later proved to have been tampered with. In some, an extra hump had been **superimposed** onto the original photo.

Monster bureau

In 1961, the Loch Ness Investigation Bureau was founded by British **naturalist** Sir Peter Scott. Its goal was to explore the loch more systematically. The Bureau gathered information on all the existing sightings. It organized a long-term watch over the loch. Nightly, teams of scientists scoured the loch with searchlights and **sonar**. They detected several large objects in the water. No one was able to identify them.

The Loch Ness Project

The Loch Ness Project was founded in 1978. It organizes field trips for students who volunteer to work at the loch. One of their tasks is to take samples of the **sediment** from the bottom. These are used for finding out more about the history of the loch. The samples may help to determine what type of creature the monster could be. The leader of the Project is naturalist Adrian Shine. After 20 years of searching, he is now convinced that there is no Loch Ness Monster to be found.

Playing tricks

*One of the problems with eyewitness accounts is that the loch itself plays tricks on the eyes. On a calm day, the steep shorelines cause shadows and reflections to form. These can make objects such as water birds, otters, boat **wakes,** and waves appear much bigger or longer than they actually are. Logs, mats of floating vegetation, and even motor boats have been mistaken for monsters. So, is the monster an **optical illusion**, or a case of mistaken identity, as many scientists suspect?*

a European otter.

Searching Underwater

For people hoping to find a monster in Loch Ness, the best place to look is, of course, under the water. If a monster does exist, this is where it would spend most of its time. Sending human divers down into the loch is risky business. The water is very cold, very deep, and very murky. Scientists have had to find other ways of exploring the loch. The two most effective methods used so far are **sonar** searching and underwater photography.

How sonar works

The word sonar stands for Sound Navigation and Ranging. A sonar machine on board a boat sends out a pulse of sound in a narrow beam. It listens for echoes as the sound bounces off objects in the water. From the time it takes for an echo to return, the machine figures out where they are. The exact location of the objects appears on a screen. Sonar can also show an object's size, shape, and speed. Some sonar machines can be towed alongside the boat to cover greater areas.

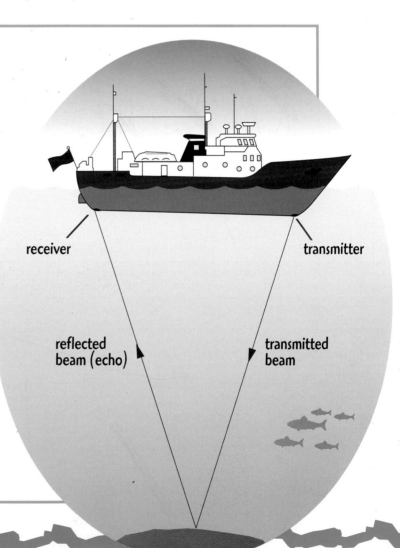

receiver

transmitter

reflected beam (echo)

transmitted beam

Sonar searching

The first scientific expedition to Loch Ness was organized in 1959 by the Natural History Museum in London. Using sonar, scientists detected a large object just below the water's surface. They tracked it as it dove to a depth of 66 feet (20 meters) and then rose back up again. The object may have been a shoal of fish. A more recent expedition was Operation Deepscan in 1987. A **flotilla** of 24 boats equipped with sonar spent a week patrolling the loch. They detected a mysterious object that they described as "the size of a large shark."

A row of sonar boats scan Loch Ness in search of a monster during Operation Deepscan in 1987. Various mysterious, and still unidentified, objects were detected in the water.

Mistaken identity?

Hundreds of sonar "hits" have been made. The sonar hits seem to show that there are large animals living in Loch Ness. But scientifically, they do not prove that there is a monster. Sonar could easily have detected large shoals of fish, rising bubbles of gas in the water, or even giant underwater waves. Some of the sonar readings, however, including three picked up by Operation Deepscan, are yet to be identified.

Underwater Photography

In 1972 and 1975, Dr. Robert Rines led a team of scientists from the Academy of Applied Science, in Massachusetts. They made a series of trips to Loch Ness. Working with the Loch Ness Investigation Bureau, they set up automatic cameras under the water. The cameras were set to flash every few seconds, or whenever their **sonar** detected moving objects. To the teams delight, several of the photographs appeared to show parts of a large creature.

In 1980, Robert Rines returned to Loch Ness. He attached an underwater camera to a frame. Taking photographs underwater is difficult because of the loch's murky water.

The flipper picture

*One of the 1972 photographs appeared to show a large, diamond-shaped flipper. The 1975 photos showed the head and body of a large creature. This led **naturalist** Sir Peter Scott to believe that the monster might have been a **plesiosaur,** a **prehistoric** reptile thought to be long **extinct**. The photographs were sent to leading **zoologists**. One scientist went so far as to say that the photos seemed to indicate the presence of large animals in the loch. But no one was able to say for sure what kind of animals they might be.*

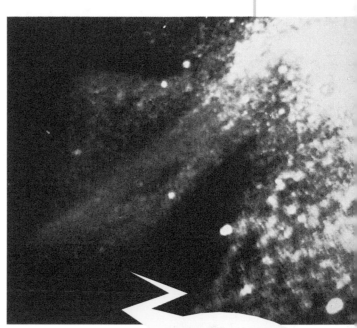

Could this be the Loch Ness Monster? Rines' famous photograph, taken in 1972, appears to show a flipper belonging to a large, creature.

Return to Loch Ness

In 1997, Robert Rines returned to Loch Ness to try to prove once and for all that something was lurking in its water. He brought along Charles Wyckoff, a photographic pioneer. Wyckoff had developed the techniques used to photograph the surface of the moon and nuclear bomb explosions. The goal was to sweep the loch using sonar. The results would be relayed to a **GPS** (Global Positioning System) on the shore. Then, the objects exact location would be pinpointed. The camera crew would follow close behind. The sonar detected several large, moving targets. The team's **marine biologist** could not explain them as shoals of fish. Taking clear photographs proved to be much harder than expected. The murky water limited visibility to a few feet. Moisture seeped in and ruined the cameras. So, the mystery remains to be solved.

What Is It?

What type of monster do eyewitnesses claim to have seen? Their reports are remarkably similar. They often describe a large, long-necked, hump-backed creature. It sometimes swims quickly with its neck raised or lowered. Sometimes it sinks beneath the water. Could it indeed be a **plesiosaur,** as Sir Peter Scott suggested? Or does the scientific evidence rule this out?

For and against

Plesiosaurs were long-necked reptiles. They lived in warm, inland seas during **prehistoric** times. They were thought to have died out some 70 million years ago, at about the same time as the dinosaurs. But there is no absolute proof that they do not still exist. Their shape certainly matches the photographs and descriptions of the Loch Ness Monster.

Scientists have used fossil remains to reconstruct the body of a plesiosaur. This model clearly shows how closely the plesiosaur matches the photographs and descriptions of Nessie.

Could a small group of plesiosaurs have escaped **extinction** in Loch Ness? If they did, could they have been overlooked by scientists? Think about these questions as if you were a scientist. First, reptiles are cold-blooded animals. They rely on the sun to warm their bodies. Could they live in the freezing water of Loch Ness? No known reptile could survive such cold. Second, the **geological** history of the loch seems to rule out plesiosaurs. During each **Ice Age**, Loch Ness was frozen solid. When the last Ice Age ended, about 12,000 years ago, it connected the loch to the sea. A shallow passage, the Ness River, was formed. Did the plesiosaurs swim from the sea to the river and then into the loch? Although this is unlikely, it is not impossible. What do you think?

Other "lost" animals

Cryptozoology is the study of cryptids, or "unknown" animals. These are animals thought to be extinct. One example is a fish called the coelacanth. Thought to have died out 70 million years ago, a living coelacanth was caught in the Indian Ocean in 1938. Scientists were amazed. If the coelacanth still exists, what about other prehistoric animals? Could there be a plesiosaur still living in Loch Ness?

a coelacanth

Mammals and Fish

If science rules out the **plesiosaur** and other reptiles, what other type of creature could the monster be? Other possible candidates are mammals and fish.

A mammal?

Some scientists think that the Loch Ness Monster might be a large mammal, such as a whale. Mammals are warm-blooded so they can adapt to the cold conditions. But the largest whales are **filter-feeders**. They eat **plankton**. Only a small amount of plankton live in Loch Ness. Therefore, the monster could not be a filter-feeder. Other mammals, such as seals, need to leave the water to breed. There have been no sightings or traces of young. If the monster does exist, it must be part of a group. It needs to breed for the species to survive. Mammals breathe air. They need to come to the surface to breathe. If the creature is a mammal, people would have the chance to see it whenever it surfaced for air.

Finding Food

*If a large creature lives in Loch Ness, it would probably eat fish. But it seems unlikely that the loch's fish supply is large enough to support a large **predator**. Despite the loch's great size, the water is poor in **nutrients**. It can't support a large food chain. The loch is dark, so few plant plankton grow in it. Therefore, there isn't enough animal plankton to eat. This means there isn't enough food for larger animals. If a monster lives in the loch, it may be very hungry.*

A fish?

If there is a large creature in Loch Ness, it is more likely to be a fish than a mammal. Some people think that it could be a giant eel or a Baltic sturgeon. Sturgeons are the largest type of freshwater fish. It is possible that the sturgeon enters the loch looking for a mate. If it does not find one, it swims out to sea again. Both types of fish can grow to more than 10 feet (3 meters) long. However, the descriptions of the monster don't match any known fish. It would help if scientists could examine a specimen, dead or alive. Even a part of the creature, such as a skeleton or skin would help solve the mystery.

Basking sharks are among the largest fish. Like whales, they feed on plankton. They can grow to be more than 36 feet (11 meters) long. In the summer, they live in British waters. They swim inshore during their annual **migration**. In winter, they disappear again. One theory is that they move into deep water to hibernate. Could this deep water be Loch Ness?

This is the mouth of a basking shark, one of the biggest fish in the sea. If scientists could prove that these creatures spend the winter in Loch Ness, the monster mystery could be solved.

Waves, Wakes, and Waterspouts

People who do not believe that the loch is home to a monster think that the answer is in the water. They look for the answer in the waves and shadows on the loch's surface, **wakes** left by passing boats, or weird weather **phenomena**. So, just how monsterlike can water be?

Waves and wakes

In rough weather, the wakes from passing boats are quickly broken up by the wind and waves. But on calm days—the days most monster sightings have been reported—the wakes last longer and look much bigger. From low down, the wake can look like a rippling row of humps moving across the water. Could these explain the many accounts of a hump-backed monster? Large waves breaking in the shallows may also be mistaken for a creature swimming.

This wake was photographed on Loch Ness in August 1996. Mysteriously, it was a clear day with no wind, and there were no boats passing nearby.

Waterspouts

Waterspouts are spinning funnels of water that are sucked up by thunder clouds passing over water. The tallest ever seen was almost a mile (1.5 kilometers) high. At sea, terrified sailors often mistook them for monsters. Water devils are smaller versions of waterspouts. They spin across the water, whipping up spray up to about ten feet (3 meters) high. British tornado and whirlwind expert Dr. Terence Meaden believes that water devils may help to explain the Loch Ness Monster mystery. Their long, tapering, funnel shape could easily be mistaken for a monster's long, thin head and neck. Water devils also cause the surface of the water to bubble and froth. Could the rings of bubbles look like a monster's humps?

Seeing things?

A mirage is an image of an object that is not really there. People have seen boats, buildings, and perhaps even monsters, as a result of these **optical illusions**. Mirages are caused by changes in temperature in different layers of air over land or water. Light rays coming from existing objects can be bent up or down as they pass through these layers. The reflection of the object is distorted. Your brain is tricked into thinking that the what you see is really there. For example, you may think you see a puddle of water on the road on a hot summer day. What you are actually seeing is a mirage of the sky. Could "Nessie" be the result of a mirage?

Monster Fakes

Many of the eyewitness sightings and photographs of the Loch Ness Monster have turned out to be fakes. Some are cases of mistaken identity. Others are hoaxes. Hoaxes are carefully planned and intended to trick people. Why do people do it? The obvious reasons are to gain fame or money. One person went as far as to suggest that the monster was an elaborate hoax made up by the Scottish Tourist Board to attract more visitors!

The surgeon's photograph

One of the most famous photographs of the Loch Ness Monster appeared in April 1934. Nicknamed "the surgeon's photograph," it was taken by London surgeon Robert Kenneth Wilson. The photo clearly showed a long neck with a tiny head, arched over the water. When the photograph was printed in the newspaper, it caused a sensation. But was it real? Many people thought so.

The most famous of all monster pictures is the so-called "surgeon's photograph." In 1994, the photograph was claimed to be a fake. But some experts have dismissed these claims. Is it a fake or is it genuine? The controversy continues.

In 1994, Loch Ness researcher Alisdair Boyd claimed that the photo was an elaborate fake. His questioning led him to Christian Spurling. Spurling confessed to helping the surgeon plan the hoax to trick the newspapers. He said that the object in the photo was, in fact, a 12 inch (30 cm) plastic neck attached to a toy submarine. From the shape of the ripples in the water, Boyd calculated the angle at which the photo had been taken. Then, Boyd lined up his camera and took some pictures of a 12 inch (30 cm) styrofoam neck that he had placed in the water. The results were almost identical. Boyd doubted the photo was real. But he is convinced that there is a monster in Loch Ness. He claims he's seen it.

Monster footprints

In December 1933, there was great excitement. A set of monster-sized footprints was discovered on the loch shore. People were eager to find out how they got there. Many people were disappointed when they found the answer. The footprints were made by something unusual—an umbrella stand made from the stuffed back foot of a hippopotamus!

What's in a name?

*Based on the **rhomboid,** or diamond, shape of the flipper in Rines' famous photograph, **naturalist** Sir Peter Scott suggested a scientific Latin name for the monster:* Nessiteras rhombopteryx. *Doubters discovered that you could rearrange the letters to read "Monster hoax by Sir Peter S"!*

Other Lake Monsters

Loch Ness is not the only lake where long-necked monsters are thought to lurk. Seemingly, monsters are everywhere. They have been sighted in about 300 lakes all over the world, from Europe to Southeast Asia. If hard proof was found for any of these, it would help in the search for the Loch Ness Monster.

Lake Okanagan, Canada

Lake Okanagan in western Canada is thought to be home to a monster called Ogopogo. Hundreds of sightings have been recorded. In July 1986, a man fishing on the lake reported, "It looked like a submarine surfacing, coming towards my boat. As it came up, we could see six humps out of the water, each one creating a wake." One woman reported almost running over it as she was water-skiing. The local Okanakane Indians have many myths about a lake serpent. When crossing the lake by canoe, legend says, travellers always took a chicken or dog to sacrifice if the monster came too close.

A lakeside model of Ogopogo, the monster in Lake Okanagan, Canada. Sightings of this monster rival those of Nessie.

Lake Champlain, Vermont

Stories of a monster in Lake Champlain, between New York and Vermont, also go back hundreds of years. Nicknamed "Champ," the monster is often described as having a long, curvy neck, with a dark body and several humps. The most convincing evidence for Champ's existence was a photograph taken in 1977. It showed a huge, long-necked creature. Despite close scientific analysis, the photo shows no sign of being faked in any way. Whether you see the monster or not, you can always munch some "Champ's chips" or listen to Champ 101.3 FM, the monster's own radio station!

This photo, taken in 1977, added fuel to the rumor that there was a monster living in Lake Champlain.

Lake Ikeda, Japan

The first photograph of "Issie," the monster in Lake Ikeda, on the island of Honshu, Japan, was taken by Mr. Matsubara in 1978. Legend says that Issie was once a beautiful white horse living by the lake. One day, a Samurai warrior took her foal away. In despair, Issie jumped into the lake, occasionally surfacing in the form of a dark, humped monster to look for her foal.

In Conclusion

So, can science really solve the mystery of the Loch Ness Monster? Despite the thousands of eyewitness accounts and photographic evidence, scientists are not convinced. Eyewitnesses are often unreliable. Photographs are easy to fake. Without solid proof, such as a skeleton, the monster seems fated to remain a myth.

Science cannot seem to solve the mystery, for now at least. It cannot prove that a large creature of some sort does not exist in Loch Ness. Can all the eyewitnesses be wrong? Many were respectable, reliable people, with no reason to make up their stories. Or was the loch itself playing tricks on them, turning boat wakes, waves, and water devils into hump-backed monsters?

Those who claim to have seen the Loch Ness Monster do not have any doubts at all. Whether science agrees or not, they believe that something large and alive is lurking in Loch Ness. After all, there are plenty of places for it to hide.

*The search for the Loch Ness Monster continues. This is a **sonar** research ship used by Project Urquhart to scan the loch in 1992. Several expeditions have come close to finding something. But what that something is, nobody yet knows.*

What do you think?

Now you know a lot about the Loch Ness Monster and the possible explanations for it. Can you draw any conclusions? Do you believe that a monster could exist? Do you have any theories of your own?

What about the eyewitness accounts? Do you think they were accurate or **optical illusions?** Could any of the photos have been real? What about the unidentified sonar "hits"? If they weren't shoals of fish, what were they? And what sort of creature could the monster be—a "lost" animal from **prehistoric** times or a known mammal or fish?

Try to keep an open mind. Remember that if scientists throughout history had not bothered to investigate everything that appeared at first to be strange or mysterious, many scientific discoveries would never have been made at all.

Glossary

animate something that is alive

cryptozoology science that studies ancient animals thought to be extinct

extinct when a species of plant or animal has died out for ever

filter-feeder animal, such as a whale or large shark, that feeds on tiny plants and animals

flotilla small group of boats

geology science that studies the history of the earth

GPS (Global Positioning System) very accurate way of finding locations on land, sea, or in the air, using information sent from satellites orbiting the earth to a small computer on the ground.

hallucination sights, sounds, or events that appear real but are not

Ice Age period in history when snow and ice covered much of the earth

marine biologist scientist who studies life in the sea

migration long journey made by some fish, birds, and mammals between their feeding and breeding grounds

mirage image of an object in the air or water that is not really there, caused by light being bent through layers of air in the atmosphere

NASA (National Aeronautics and Space Administration) the organization that runs the space program in the United States

naturalist scientist who studies the natural world

nutrients substances that provide food and nourishment for living things

optical illusion vision or image that tricks the eye into seeing something that is not there

phenomenon remarkable or unexplained happening

plankton tiny plants and animals that drift on the surface of water and provide food for other animals

plesiosaur long-necked prehistoric reptile

predator any animal that survives by hunting other animals

prehistoric before recorded time

rhomboid diamond-shaped

sediment layer of mud, sand, and rock that lies on the bottom of a lake or river

sonar (Sound Navigation Ranging) device used to locate and map underwater objects by sending out sound waves and picking up their echoes with a microphone

superimposed placed on top of something else, such as something that is added to an existing photograph

wake trail left on the surface of the water by a moving ship or boat

zoologist scientist who studies animals

More Books to Read

Abels, Harriette S. *Loch Ness Monster.* Parsippany, NJ: Silver Burdett Press. 1987.

Landau, Elaine. *The Loch Ness Monster.* Brookfield, Conn: Millbrook Press, 1993.

Steffens, Bradley, *The Loch Ness Monster.* San Diego, Cal: Lucent Books, 1995.

Index